THE
RED SEA
RULES
STUDY GUIDE

Take the Journey from Panic to Praise

Morris Proctor

©2014 Robert J. Morgan Books • Nashville, TN 37214

Contents

INTRODUCTION

Take the Journey from Panic to Praise

Hello, my name is Morris Proctor. I'm a friend of Robert J. Morgan, author of the book, *The Red Sea Rules.*

I invite you to join me on a journey—a journey through the Red Sea.

Centuries ago, God's people, the Israelites, served as slaves to Egyptian authorities. To deliver them, God providentially directed His children out of Egypt to the edge of the Red Sea. Fearing loss of their work force, Egyptian armies pursued their runaway slaves. With waves of water crashing in front of them and teams of soldiers chasing behind them, the children of Israel found themselves between the sword and the sea. To them, their only two choices were submitting to slavery or succumbing to death in the sea. Fear and panic bellowed from the Israelites as they complained to their leader, Moses, "What have you done to us?" (Exodus 14:1–12).

Then God...

Then God parted the waters allowing His people to journey to victory through the Red Sea. When the last Israelite was safely on the other side, the walls of water collapsed onto the Egyptian militia. In mere moments, the Red Sea went from being Israel's destruction to Israel's deliverance (14:21–29).

Seeing the great power of God, the Israelites' fear turned to faith. Their panic became praise (14:31—15:20).

Please note, their transformation didn't just happen. They first followed the rules— The Red Sea Rules. They applied the principles. They took the steps in a journey.

The above episode isn't just an event from the past. It's an example for the present. Allow me to explain.

My close friend, Rob Morgan, experienced a difficult season of life several years ago. Engulfed with anxiety bordering on panic, he opened his Bible to Exodus 14. There he read the above account of the journey through the Red Sea. But rather than reading mere historic facts, Rob discovered dynamic principles: **The Red Sea Rules**. He saw 10 God-given strategies for difficult times. Being a practitioner before a preacher, he applied these ten strategies to his own difficult times. He too experienced victory.

This ten-step journey through the Red Sea took God's people in the past and Rob in the present, from fear to faith—from panic to praise. And the really good news is, you and I can also experience this same transformation in our difficult times.

So I ask you, will you join me on a journey through the Red Sea, moving from panic to praise?

In all likelihood we've never met, but I know one thing about you: you're either encountering or soon will encounter a problem, a challenge, a difficulty in life.

Jesus cautioned us in John 16:33 "here on earth you will have many trials and sorrows" (NLT).

James prepared us in James 1:2, by saying, "when [not if] you meet trials of various kinds" (ESV).

You and I frequently come face to face with our own Red Sea. It just has a different name:

- *Strained Relationship Sea*

- *Financial Stress Sea*

- *Prodigal Child (or Parent) Sea*

- *Failing Health Sea*

- *Problems at Work Sea*

- "Insert Your Problem Here" Sea

Regardless of what we call it, we face times that seem to overwhelm us. We see no way out. We want to give up, give out, and give in. Fear freezes us. Panic paralyzes us.

There's an alternative, though. It's the ten-step journey through our Red Sea.

Each of the ten Red Sea Rules becomes a step in our journey:

1. Realize that God means for you to be where you are.

2. Be more concerned for God's glory than your relief.

3. Acknowledge your enemy, but keep your eyes on the Lord.

4. Pray!

5. Stay calm and confident, and give God time to work.

6. When unsure, just take the next logical step by faith.

7. Envision God's enveloping presence.

8. Trust God to deliver in His own unique way.

9. View your current crisis as a faith builder for the future.

10. Don't forget to praise Him.

Please view each lesson as a mini-journey unto itself, with all ten combining for the complete excursion, crossing, or itinerary. To understand the structure of each lesson, think through four stages of taking a trip.

For each step I'll guide you through a four-part lesson:

PREVIEW THE JOURNEY

When taking a trip, we begin by **previewing** our trip. We determine where we're going. The beach? The mountains? The desert? We then map it. We chart our course. We read the brochures deciding what we'll see. Likewise, as we **preview** each step of our Red Sea journey, we'll focus on the biblical text, discovering the actual step the children of Israel took. And of course, the same step we're about to take.

PREPARE FOR THE JOURNEY

Having previewed our trip, we must now **prepare** for our trip. Do we need to pack sandals or boots? Surf boards or snow boards? It would be bad to arrive in Florida only to discover we brought parkas and mittens. In like manner, before we take a step in our Red Sea journey, we must **prepare**. Difficulties are hard enough without increasing the pain due to our lack of preparation. During each step's **preparation**, you'll have the opportunity to do some soul searching, readying yourself for the actual step in the journey.

PROCEED ON THE JOURNEY

After previewing and preparing for the trip, we finally **proceed** on the journey. We really get to swim, surf, or ski. This of course is where each lesson leads: **proceed** on the journey. We actually have to take a step of faith and apply the Red Sea Rule. We have to live out the principle. In each lesson you'll have the opportunity to prayerfully commit to take the next step of the journey.

PONDER THE JOURNEY

Unfortunately, our greatest journeys are quickly forgotten. With each step, we need to **ponder** the journey—to mentally process and physically record events, thoughts, and emotions. At the end of this guide, blank space is provided where you can
ponder the journey and journal the story of your own Red Sea experience.

Along the way, please keep in mind some helpful hints:

- Make sure to carefully read all of the Scripture references in each lesson. Our transformation from panic to praise occurs when we apply biblical, rather than self-help principles.

- Also, try to honestly answer each question. Some questions and answers may be uncomfortable or even painful. True transformation comes, however, only when we're honest with ourselves and our Lord.

- In addition, please don't rush the journey. You may spend extended time on one step. Just because we fill in the blanks doesn't mean we've taken the step. Allow the Lord time to process each step within you.

- Finally, remember the journey through the Red Sea is not a one-time trip. We'll repeat and relive these ten steps for each challenge we face in life. Hopefully, as we mature in Christ, the journey will get more familiar and a bit easier, but it will be a repeated journey nonetheless.

Ready to join me in taking the ten-step journey through the Red Sea?

Let's start here:

What Red Sea are you currently facing?

_____

_____

What are your reactions in the midst of this difficulty? Fear? Anger? Panic? Depression?

_____

_____

_____

_____

Will you take whatever faith you have, even if it's small as a mustard seed, and place it in a God who wants to guide you through your Red Sea (Luke 17:5–6)?

_____

If you're ready, by faith, to take a journey through your Red Sea then carefully read Exodus 14 at least twice and pray the following prayer:

Heavenly Father.

You see better than I the challenge I'm currently facing. You also clearly see my condition. On good days I have hope. On bad days I'm hopeless. Right now I don't have great faith, but I know You're a great God. You took Your children in the past from panic to praise. Will You do the same for me? By Your grace and power I'm embarking on this journey through my Red Sea. Lord I believe; help my unbelief. Make me into a trusting, praising child of Yours.

In Jesus' name, Amen.

RULE #1

Realize that God means for you to be where you are.

The older I get, the more convinced I am that life is hard! Just today as I was writing this lesson:

- My son informed me he has to have another shoulder surgery (third one in three years)

- My cousin ran his car through a telephone pole

- My friend called telling me he's bankrupt

Yes, life is tough. Red Seas come in all shapes and sizes. I don't need to tell you that, though. You have your own Red Sea.

Again for clarity, what's the Red Sea you're focusing on for this journey?

_____

_____

_____

_____

I don't know about you, but when I'm stuck between a rock and a hard place, hemmed in between the sword and the sea, I want to know WHY.

Why is life so hard? Why do problems persist? Why do we encounter these Red Seas?

_____

_____

_____

_____

We'll probably never know all of the reasons, but as we start our trek through the Red Sea, we begin with Step #1 which is:

Realize that God means for you to be where you are.

Yes, you read that correctly. God isn't surprised by the challenges in our lives. Rob writes:

> *Our whole perspective changes when, finding ourselves in a hard place, we realize the Lord has either placed us there or allowed us to be there, perhaps for reasons presently known only to Himself.*

What's your initial reaction to Rob's statement?

That God is in control and he has put us
where we are for a reason

Let's explore this first step in more detail.

PREVIEW THE JOURNEY

Read Rule #1 in *The Red Sea Rules*.

Read carefully Exodus 14:1–2.

Who directed the children of Israel to camp by the sea?

The Lord

Rewrite Exodus 14:1–2 in your own words.

The Lord to Moses: Camp by the sea near
Pbi Hahiroth, between Migdal & the sea
across form Baal Zephon

In all seriousness, was God aware of the depths of the sea? The approaching Egyptian armies? The predicament His people would face because of His directions? Explain.

Yes, because God has control of
everything

Did God make a mistake when He deliberately led His people into a cul-de-sac between hostile hills, to the edge of a sea too deep to be forded and too wide to be crossed? Explain.

No God will never put us in a situation that we can't get out of

Rewrite Rule #1 in your own words; use personal pronouns (I, me, my, etc.).

God means for me to be where I am because He has work on me yet and will never leave me or forsake me!

PREPARE FOR THE JOURNEY

So we see from Exodus 14:1–2, God led His people to the shore of the Red Sea. Perhaps that challenge was just for them. Surely it's not the norm for God's people to face hardship? If we're to be prepared for our struggles we must know the answer.

Reread page 9 where Rob lists people from the Bible who encountered trials. Was this Red Sea event a single biblical occurrence of God permitting problems in people's lives or does Scripture contain other examples? List any others you can think of.

Saul/Paul had his thorn

What do John 16:33, James, 1:2, and 1 Peter 4:12 teach about difficulties in life?

In this world I will have trouble Consider it pare joy when you face trials do not be surprised at the trials

What do Genesis 50:15–21, Job 1:6–12, and Isaiah 6 teach about the relationship between the sovereignty of God and the suffering of people?

God intends suffering for God
God allows suffering and uses for good

In light of the above verses, if Rob wanted to add you and your Red Sea to page 9, what would he write?

Sometimes, however, our problems result from our own bad choices. What then? Read Psalm 103:12, Proverbs 28:13, and 1 John 1:8–9 and record your findings about forgiveness and fellowship with God.

We do have bad choices and don't follow Gods
will for us, he will forgive us if we confess
those sins.

Read about Peter's bad choices in Luke 22:54–62. According to Luke 22:31–32, John 21:15–17, and Acts 2:14, 37–41 was God able to lead Peter through his Bad Choices Sea? Explain.

yes

In Romans 8:28 what does the phrase "all things" include? Exclude?

includes everything, excludes nothing

If your Red Sea resulted from your own bad choices, what have you learned from the above verses?

_____

_____

_____

_____

PROCEED ON THE JOURNEY

We clearly see from the Bible that God is neither worried nor weakened when His children, including you and me, encounter troubles and trials. Knowing that God is in control of our lives regardless of what befalls us is not only the first step of our journey, but arguably the most important. Subsequent steps that include faith, prayer, and praise are virtually impossible to take unless we believe in an all-powerful, loving God.

Be honest, how have you been initially reacting to your Red Sea? Circle the emotions that apply:

anxiousness   nervousness   fear   regret   uncertainty   frustration

panic   depression   sadness   despondency   anger

How can embracing Rule #1 affect your response?

_____

_____

_____

_____

PONDER THE JOURNEY

In light of Rule #1, record a journal entry that includes reactions and your intended response to what you've learned. Blank journal pages are provided for Step #1 beginning on Page 65 in the back of this study guide.

Heavenly Father,

Through my mistakes, the choices of others, and Your providence, I am where I am. I'm facing this challenge. I confess I'm full of fear, worry, and panic. But I don't want to be in this emotional, spiritual chaotic state. I want to praise You in all things and at all times. To get there I must realize that You mean for me to be where I am. I recognize Your sovereignty. I praise You for being a God who never sleeps or grows weary. You're fully aware of my circumstances. I choose to trust You.

In Jesus' name, Amen

And we know that all things work together for good to those who love God, to those who are the called according to His purpose. (NKJV)

Romans 8:28

RULE #2

Be more concerned for God's glory than for your relief.

I recently spoke with a young man who recounted a list of problems he has already faced even at a young age:

- His father went AWOL

- His health is poor

- He wrecked his car

- He dropped out of college, twice

- He lost three jobs

He then asked me, *Why has all of this happened to me?*

Can you relate? In the midst of your Red Sea challenge have you asked similar questions? Please circle a question below that most compares to what you've been asking.

- What have I done to deserve this?

- Why me?

- If God loves me, why this?

- How can I get out of this mess?

Rob writes:

> *These are natural questions, but they may be the wrong ones to ask.*

Learning to ask the right question in the midst of trials is actually Red Sea Rule #2 and the second step in our journey through the Red Sea:

Be more concerned for God's glory than your relief.

PREVIEW THE JOURNEY

Read Rule #2 in *The Red Sea Rules*.

Slowly read Exodus 14:3–4, 10–12.

To clearly understand this second step we must realize there were two viewpoints regarding the Red Sea: God's and His people's.

According to Exodus 14:3–4 why did God lead His people to the edge of the sea?

_____

_____

_____

God intended to *get glory* or *gain honor* from the Red Sea experience. What does this mean?

_____

_____

_____

_____

Is God's desire to *get glory* or *gain honor* motivated by neediness, narcissism, or egomania on His part? Why or why not?

_____

_____

_____

_____

What is the meaning of the phrase *the Egyptians shall know I am the Lord*?

_____

_____

_____

What is the relationship between *get glory* and *the Egyptians shall know I am the Lord*?

_____

_____

_____

_____

How could the journey through the Red Sea result in *getting glory* and *knowing God is the Lord*?

_____

_____

_____

_____

Circle every occurrence of the words *we* and *us* in Exodus 14:11–12 below.

> *Then they said to Moses, "Because there were no graves in Egypt, have you taken us away to die in the wilderness? Why have you so dealt with us, to bring us up out of Egypt? Is this not the word that we told you in Egypt, saying, 'Let us alone that we may serve the Egyptians'? For it would have been better for us to serve the Egyptians than that we should die in the wilderness." (NKJV)*

As the children of Israel found themselves between the sword and the sea, what were they most concerned about?

_____

_____

_____

_____

Two clearly defined perspectives emerge from Exodus 14: God-focused and self-focused.

Explain the Exodus 14:2–3 God-focused perspective in the midst of trials:

_____

_____

_____

Explain the Exodus 14:11–12 self-focused perspective in the midst of trials:

_____

_____

_____

_____

Based on Exodus 15:1–3, did God's people change their perspective? Explain.

_____

_____

_____

_____

Using personal pronouns (I, me, my, etc.) rewrite Rule #2 in your own words.

_____

_____

PREPARE FOR THE JOURNEY

Exodus 14 is but one of many passages demonstrating God's desire to change our perspective on life's problems. For instance, on numerous occasions Jesus both explained and exemplified this truth. In the following passages describe both the God-focused and self-focused perspective:

John 9:1–3

Self-focused:

_____

_____

_____

God-focused:

_____

_____

_____

John 11:1–4, 17–27

Self-focused:

_____

_____

_____

God-focused:

_____

_____

_____

John 12:27–28

Self-focused:

_____

_____

_____

God-focused:

_____

_____

_____

Using personal pronouns (I, me, my, etc.) rewrite Psalm 115:1 in your own words.

_____

_____

_____

When God gets glory from life's dilemmas does that mean He always removes our problems or stops the pain? Use Hebrews 11:36–40 to help with your answer.

_____

_____

_____

_____

Our natural mind tells us if we want to fix the problem we must first and foremost focus on ourselves. Is there, however, a spiritual paradigm that says otherwise? Explain your answer based on Matthew 16:24.

_____

_____

_____

_____

I mentioned that Rob is my friend but he is also my father in the faith. Years ago as a college freshman athlete I thought my world was falling apart:

- I injured my knee

- I broke up with my girlfriend

- I lost interest in school

I stumbled into Rob's office looking for help and relief. He instructed me to pull my shirt over my eyes and then asked me, *What do you see?* I responded, *I see everything in the room, but everything is fuzzy.* He then hit me right between the eyes with these words:

> *That's your problem. You're looking at your life through your own skin. Have you ever thought about what God wants to do in and through your life?*

For the first time in my life I realized it's not all about me. There's something more to life than just what I want.

PROCEED ON THE JOURNEY

Rob writes:

> *The next time you're overwhelmed, instead of asking, "How can I get out of this mess?" try asking, "How can God be glorified in this situation?" One's perspective is entirely changed by the spiritual realities behind this approach.*

How might God *get glory* or *gain honor* in your Red Sea?

_____

_____

_____

_____

Describe if and how your perspective on your Red Sea has changed because of Rule #2.

_____

_____

_____

_____

PONDER THE JOURNEY

In light of Rule #2, record a journal entry that includes reactions and your intended response to what you've learned. Blank journal pages are provided for Step #2 beginning on Page 67 in the back of this study guide.

Heavenly Father,

I freely admit my first reaction to this challenge was: "Fix it. Stop it. Make it go away". Now Lord I want You to be glorified through it. I don't fully understand how that will take place, but I humbly ask You to reveal that answer to me. Manifest Your character in and through my life so that others may see and know that You are the Lord.

In Jesus' name, Amen.

Now My soul is troubled, and what shall I say? 'Father, save Me from this hour'? But for this purpose I came to this hour. Father, glorify Your name." (NKJV)

John 12:27–28

THE
RED SEA
RULES
STUDY GUIDE

RULE #3

Acknowledge your enemy, but keep your eyes on the Lord.

As a boy I spent a lot of time at my grandmother's house in the country. My cousins and I ran through the large fields. We climbed trees. We jumped logs. All was grand except for one thing. My grandmother kept chained in the yard a large, solid black, ferocious dog named—Satan. His growls and snarls sent shivers up and down our spines. His sole purpose in life was to rob us of fun. What if we got too close? What if he broke his chain? The knowledge of his presence always lurked in our minds curtailing our joy and laughter.

Likewise, as we seek to enjoy God and glorify Him, we have an adversary, the devil prowling around like a roaring lion seeking someone to devour (1 Peter 5:8). As we endeavor to experience the abundant life in Jesus, Satan tries to steal, kill, and destroy us (John 10:10).

So as you face your Red Sea keep in mind what Rob writes:

> *If you're in a tough situation right now, suffering pain, worry, anguish, or illness, the devil is undoubtedly behind it to a greater or lesser degree.*

How then should we respond to the knowledge of a real enemy out to destroy us? That's Step #3 in our journey:

Acknowledge Your Enemy but Keep Your Eyes on the Lord

PREVIEW THE JOURNEY

Read Exodus 14:5–9.

Read Rule #3 in *The Red Sea Rules*.

After the Israelites left Egypt, getting their first taste of freedom, what did Pharaoh do (Exodus 14:6–7)?

_____

_____

What was one of the reasons Pharaoh pursued God's people (Exodus 14:5)?

_____

_____

_____

_____

Describe the forces with which Pharaoh tracked the Israelites (Exodus 14:6–9)?

_____

_____

_____

_____

Rob suggests there are parallels between Pharaoh and Satan.

According to 1 Peter 5:8 is Satan pursuing God's people?

_____

_____

_____

_____

In light of John 10:10 why might the devil seek to war against the children of God?

_____

_____

_____

_____

Is Satan alone in his attacks against Christians? Who else is involved?

_____

_____

_____

_____

How did the Israelites react when they saw the Egyptian armies (Exodus 14:10)?

_____

_____

_____

_____

What was Moses' advice for the fearful pilgrims (Exodus 14:13–14)?

_____

_____

_____

_____

According to Ephesians 6:13–18 how are Christians to protect themselves against the attacks of the enemy?

_____

_____

_____

_____

Using personal pronouns (I, me, my, etc.) rewrite Rule #3 in your own words.

_____

_____

_____

_____

PREPARE FOR THE JOURNEY

The apostle Paul on the frontline of Christian life and ministry didn't hesitate to ascribe to Satan numerous hardships and battles. Using the following verses, describe some of the attacks from the adversary.

Acts 13:8–10: _____

_____

2 Corinthians 12:1–7: _____

_____

1 Thessalonians 2:17–18: _____

_____

1 Corinthians 7:1–5: _____

_____

1 Corinthians 10:14–20: _____

_____

2 Corinthians 2:5–11: _____

_____

2 Corinthians 11:12–14: _____

_____

Ephesians 4:26–27: _____

_____

1 Timothy 5:14–15: _____

_____

Do you believe that your Red Sea could be an attack from the enemy? Why or why not?

_____

_____

_____

_____

What are you thinking and feeling when you consider the fact that you may be under enemy attack?

_____

_____

_____

What can you learn about attacks from the enemy in Job 1:6–12?

_____

_____

_____

According to Genesis 3:15, John 12:31, Colossians 2:15 and Hebrews 2:14, what is the most important truth to remember about Satan?

_____

_____

_____

In light of the cross, what should our posture be toward Satan? Consider Ephesians 6:11, James 4:7, and 1 Peter 5:8–9.

_____

_____

_____

PROCEED ON THE JOURNEY

We can easily make two mistakes as we contemplate the activity of the adversary in our lives. We can ascribe too much to him, seeing a demon behind every bush. We can ascribe too little to him, seeing no demon behind any bush.

What biblical balance will you strike as you move forward in the journey through your Red Sea?

_____

_____

_____

How do you plan to put on the armor of God and resist the devil?

_____

_____

_____

_____

PONDER THE JOURNEY

In light of Rule #3, record a journal entry that includes reactions and your intended response to what you've learned. Blank journal pages are provided for Step #3 beginning on Page 69 in the back of this study guide.

Heavenly Father,

I realize I have an enemy who is seeking to separate me from the abundant life I have in Jesus. But I know this enemy has been judged through the cross. Therefore, I will put on the armor You have provided so I can stand against the one on the loose while he awaits execution. Give me wisdom to neither ignore nor obsess about my adversary.

In Jesus' name, Amen.

Therefore submit to God. Resist the devil and he will flee from you. (NKJV)

James 4:7

RULE #4

Pray!

In a recent pastoral phone call, a woman tearfully described her son's history of drug abuse. After months of staying clean, he went missing. No phone calls to family members informing them of his whereabouts. No text messages to his friends saying he was fine. He just left. I never will forget his mother's worried words*: I have never prayed in my life. But when I couldn't find my son, I just started praying. God help him! God help me!*

Nothing encourages prayer more than pain!

As you continue your personal pilgrimage through your own Red Sea you've come to Rule #4:

Pray!

Have you been praying as the walls of life collapsed around you? If so, summarize one of your typical prayers.

_____

_____

_____

_____

In this fourth step of our journey we'll focus on one type of petition, which Rob calls crisis-prayer.

PREVIEW THE JOURNEY

Read Rule #4 in *The Red Sea Rules*.

Slowly read Exodus 14:10 three times.

Three verbs summarize the actions of the people of Israel in Exodus 14:10. They:

- Lifted up their eyes (saw)
- Feared greatly
- Cried out to the Lord

What did the Israelites see?

_____

_____

_____

_____

Why were the Israelites fearful?

_____

_____

_____

_____

What did the approaching armies motivate the Israelites to do?

_____

_____

_____

_____

Is there a stair-stepped relationship between see—fear—cry? If so, describe it below.

_____

_____

_____

Rewrite *cried out to the Lord* several times using various synonyms.

_____

_____

What do you believe was the substance or content of their cries? What did they want?

_____

_____

_____

_____

According to Exodus 14:11–12 do you believe the people prayed in faith?

_____

_____

_____

_____

Even though their prayers may have been solely motivated by fear and lacked single-minded faith, do you believe God heard the cries of His people? Please read Nehemiah 9:9–11 before you explain your answer.

_____

_____

_____

_____

Rewrite Rule #4 in your own words.

_____

_____

_____

PREPARE FOR THE JOURNEY

Rob draws a distinction between quiet-time prayers and crisis-time prayers. Please define both types of prayers based upon Matthew 6:6 and Joshua 24:7.

_____

_____

_____

In Luke 11:1–4 Jesus gives us a pattern for prayer that's very fitting for our habitual quiet-time praying. The urgent nature of crisis-time prayers, however, sometimes necessitates nothing more than, *God help!*

Using the verses below, describe the crisis-times prayer contained in each passage:

1 Samuel 1:9–13: _____

_____

Jonah 2:1–2: _____

_____

Psalm 107:4–6: _____

_____

Matthew 8:23–27:_____

_____

Mark 5:22–23: _____

_____

Hebrews 4:16: _____

_____

Study carefully Peter's cry for help in Matthew 14:30 noticing words we have seen before in Exodus 14:10: *saw*, *afraid*, and *cried out*. In your own words explain Peter's crisis-time prayer.

_____

_____

_____

_____

_____

_____

Does God welcome crisis-time praying? Base your answer on 1 Peter 5:6–7.

_____

_____

_____

Define the *earnest* praying that Rob mentions in "United and Unfeigned".

_____

_____

_____

PROCEED ON THE JOURNEY

The Bible teaches by both precept and practice two broad types of praying: quiet-time praying to enhance fellowship with God and crisis-time praying to receive help from God. If you're new to the faith, you may not be familiar with the phrase "quiet time", which refers to a daily devotional time set aside for worship and fellowship with the Lord through prayer and Scripture reading.

Evaluate your quiet-time praying both *quantitatively* and *qualitatively*. In other words, how much time do you spend praying daily? How engaged, sincere, and earnest are you in these daily prayer times? Also describe any changes you would like to make in this area.

_____

_____

_____

If you were feeling "guilty" or hesitant about crisis-time praying, do you now see this is a biblical practice? Explain.

_____

_____

_____

Write out a prayer that is befitting of the Red Sea journey you're currently on.

_____

_____

_____

_____

PONDER THE JOURNEY

In light of Rule #4, record a journal entry that includes reactions and your intended response to what you've learned. Blank journal pages are provided for Step #4 beginning on Page 71 in the back of this study guide.

Heavenly Father,

Thank You for the invitation to come boldly to You to obtain mercy in my time of need. Thank You for allowing me to cast my cares upon You. You see my crisis. You know my need. Help me!

In Jesus' name, Amen.

Let us therefore come boldly to the throne of grace, that we may obtain mercy and find grace to help in time of need. (NKJV)

Hebrews 4:16

RULE #5

Stay calm and confident, and give God time to work.

A phone call recently interrupted my peaceful lunch break. The trembling, tearful voice on the other end immediately began and continued nonstop for five minutes: Morris…

- I'm behind on my bills

- My boss is demanding

- My adult son living at home won't get a job

- My car won't run

- My health is failing

- I'm not eating

- …

The person talking was hyperventilating and I was out of breath just listening. I finally interrupted, *Slow down. Take a deep breath. Let's examine these one by one.*

It's so easy when life presents challenges to panic. Lose control. Obsess about everything at once.

Has your personal Red Sea produced a panic prone reaction from you? Please describe.

_____

_____

_____

_____

Our next step, Rule #5, on the journey through the Red Sea deals with this very scenario:

Stay calm and confident, and give God time to work.

PREVIEW THE JOURNEY

Read Rule #5 in *The Red Sea Rules*.

Read Exodus 14:13–14.

What three instructions did Moses give the people of God in Exodus 14:13?

_____

_____

_____

_____

Using your best creative writing skills, describe the fearful scene. What influenced their fear? What did their fear-filled reaction look like?

_____

_____

_____

_____

In light of the situation, was their fearful reaction understandable? Why or why not?

_____

_____

_____

_____

Explain what Moses meant when he told the Israelites to *stand firm*.

_____

_____

_____

_____

Moses proclaimed phrases such as, *See the salvation of the Lord, He will work for you today,* and *The Lord will fight for you.* What was he trying to get the Israelites to comprehend?

_____

_____

_____

_____

At the end of Exodus 14:14, Moses told the people *you only have to remain silent* (ESV) or *you shall hold your peace* (NKJV). What was he instructing God's people to do or not do?

_____

_____

_____

_____

Using personal pronouns (I, me, my, etc.) rewrite Rule #5 in your own words.

_____

_____

_____

_____

 PREPARE FOR THE JOURNEY

On close examination, Rule #5, based on Exodus 14:13–14, consists of three separate elements:

- Stay calm (*fear not*)

- Stay confident (*stand firm*)

- Give God time to work (*see the salvation of the Lord, he will work for you, the Lord will fight for you, be silent*)

Rob states how many times the phrases *fear not* and *do not be afraid* occur in the Bible. He also quotes different writers who say Christians shouldn't be fearful regardless of the situation. Why do you agree or disagree with the writers?

_____

_____

_____

_____

When fear is present, what are we focusing on?

_____

_____

_____

Rob says that fear is an emotion that needs to be controlled. How do we control emotions?

_____

_____

_____

The positive counterpart to the negative *fear not* is *stand firm*. What are we focusing on when we *stand firm*?

_____

_____

_____

How do we improve our ability to *stand firm*?

_____

_____

_____

A natural tendency when a problem arises is to fix it! Control it! Rob encourages us, however, to *give God time to work* based on phrases such as *see the salvation of the Lord, he will work for you, the Lord will fight for you,* and *be silent.*

According to Genesis 15:1–6 and 16:1–4, do you believe Abraham was trying to control a situation? Why or why not?

_____

_____

_____

Do you believe Peter's action in John 18:4–11 was an attempt to fix a problem? Why or why not?

_____

_____

_____

Based on Genesis 1:26; 3:5, 22, do you believe there is a theological basis for trying to control our circumstances? When is it an appropriate excercise of God-given dominion? When is it sinful?

_____

_____

_____

In as much detail as possible describe what's happening inside of you when you feel the urge to control or fix a problem?

_____

_____

_____

Rob likens *giving God time to work* to the biblical concept of *waiting on God*. Read these verses and then in your own words explain the concept of *waiting on God*: Psalm 27:14; 33:20; 37:7–8; 38:15; 39:7.

_____

_____

_____

How do we move from *controlling* to *waiting*?

_____

_____

_____

_____

PROCEED ON THE JOURNEY

With 1 being *fearful* and 10 being *standing firm* where are you on the scale with your Red Sea? Explain your answer.

_____

_____

_____

With 1 being *trying to control the situation* and 10 being *waiting on God* where are you on the scale with your Red Sea? Explain your answer.

_____

_____

_____

According to Rule #5 what do you now see as a biblical response to your Red Sea?

_____

_____

_____

_____

PONDER THE JOURNEY

In light of Rule #5, record a journal entry that includes reactions and your intended response to what you've learned. Blank journal pages are provided for Step #5 beginning on Page 73 in the back of this study guide.

Heavenly Father,

When problems arise I sense I'm losing control. I panic and become afraid. To alleviate my fear I try to control and fix the problems. I now see I need to slow down, place faith in You, allowing You to guide me and control the situation. By Your grace and power may this truly become a reality in my life.

In Jesus' name, Amen.

Our soul waits for the LORD; He is our help and our shield. (NKJV)

Psalm 33:20

THE
RED SEA
RULES
STUDY GUIDE

RULE #6

When unsure, just take the next logical step by faith.

I know a middle-aged businessman who has believed for 30 years he should become a pastor, but he doesn't pursue the calling. He underlines in his Bible verses God uses to communicate his life's work. His friends in whom he confides encourage him to be a pastor. He's unfulfilled in business. His work strains his family. Yet, he doesn't change course into pastoral work. The reason, he claims, is because he doesn't want to miss God's leading. So he does nothing.

As the cliché goes, he suffers from the *paralysis of analysis*.

In your Red Sea experience, have you, for any reason, refused to take a step of action? Explain.

_____

_____

_____

_____

We'll never journey through our Red Sea unless we take another step and apply Rule #6:

When unsure, just take the next logical step by faith.

PREVIEW THE JOURNEY

Read Rule #6 in *The Red Sea Rules*.

Read Exodus 14:15 several times.

According to Exodus 14:15, what did God tell Moses to instruct the Israelites to do?

_____

_____

35

The same Hebrew word translated *go forward* is also translated throughout the Old Testament as *journeyed, moved, set out, left,* and *departed.*

If you have easy access to multiple Bible translations/versions, record various wordings of the specific instruction from the Lord.

_____

_____

_____

_____

Rephrase God's specific command in your own words.

_____

_____

_____

_____

In Rule #5 Rob emphasizes waiting on the Lord. Here in Rule #6 he encourages us to take a step. Do you see a contradiction? Why or why not?

_____

_____

_____

_____

Who is giving the command to *go forward?*

_____

How do the commands *be silent* (Exodus 14:14) and g*o forward* (Exodus 14:15) relate?

_____

_____

_____

_____

PREPARE FOR THE JOURNEY

We must avoid two extremes as we journey through our Red Sea: reacting impulsively out of fear and refusing to move even if God shows the way.

Obeying God's directions is paramount in moving through the Red Sea. Based on the verses below, how might God communicate His will for our lives?

Luke 4:4, 8, 12: _____

_____

Acts 16:6–7: _____

_____

Proverbs 15:22: _____

_____

2 Corinthians 2:12–13: _____

_____

Acts 18:1–3, 6–8: _____

_____

How far in advance does God usually reveal His will for our lives? Base your answer on the following verses: Luke 11:3; 2 Corinthians 4:16.

_____

_____

_____

_____

Rob explains:

> It is axiomatic [obvious or self-evident] that God generally leads His children step-by-step, provides for us day by day, and cares for us moment by moment.

What principle for living does Jesus communicate in Matthew 6:34?

_____

_____

_____

_____

What does Rob mean by this statement he writes:

> *I've decided that sometimes plodding is better than plotting when it comes to finding God's will.*

_____

_____

_____

_____

What does Proverbs 3:5–6 teach about faith and God's will?

_____

_____

_____

_____

Reread Rob's confession of procrastination under "Step by Step" and the question he learned to ask himself regarding his problems:

> *What little step can I take right now toward addressing this?*

Do you see a conflict between Proverbs 3:5–6 and Rob's question? Why or why not?

_____

_____

_____

_____

PROCEED ON THE JOURNEY

I confess that I tend to be *an all or nothing* person. I will do everything when I know all or I will do nothing until I know everything.

As you're journeying through your Red Sea, do you struggle with the *all or nothing* mentality? Why or why not?

_____

_____

_____

_____

Do you believe there's a *next logical step* you're to be taking regarding your Red Sea? If so describe it in detail.

_____

_____

_____

_____

Regarding the *next logical step*, are you procrastinating in taking it? If so, why?

_____

_____

_____

_____

PONDER THE JOURNEY

In light of Rule #6, record a journal entry that includes reactions and your intended response to what you've learned. Blank journal pages are provided for Step #6 beginning on Page 75 in the back of this study guide.

Heavenly Father,

I confess as I consider my Red Sea that sometimes I'm like a wave, up and down. Some days I want to spring into action fixing everything. Other days I want to retreat into solitude doing nothing. Calm me down so I can listen for Your voice. When I hear You, I want to obey without procrastination.

In Jesus' name, Amen

Trust in the LORD with all your heart, And lean not on your own understanding; In all your ways acknowledge Him, And He shall direct your paths. (NKJV)

Proverbs 3:5–6

RULE #7

Envision God's enveloping presence.

In a conversation with a man defending his reason for not becoming a Christian, he said, *At work I've watched people going through tough times. Some are Christians; some are not. They all act the same. I expect Christians to respond differently to the problems of life. Isn't God supposed to be with them?*

Let's not debate the accuracy of his observation since he was trying to justify his unbelief. His statement, however, underscores an important truth: *I expect Christians to respond differently to the problems of life. Isn't God supposed to be with them?*

Describe expected *similarities* between Christians' and non-Christians' reactions to life's trials?

_____

_____

_____

_____

Describe expected *differences* between Christians' and non-Christians' reactions to life's trials?

_____

_____

_____

_____

As we continue our journey through our Red Sea, one marked difference should manifest as we apply Rule #7.

Envision God's enveloping presence.

PREVIEW THE JOURNEY

Read Rule #7 in *The Red Sea Rules*.

Read Exodus 14:19–20 several times, using different Bible versions if necessary, until you clearly understand what's taking place.

Rewrite Exodus 14:19–20 in your own words.

_____

_____

_____

_____

Define the theological term Rob uses to describe the *angel of God* mentioned in Exodus 14:19.

_____

_____

_____

_____

So who is the *angel of God*?

_____

Describe what the *angel of God* and *pillar of cloud* did differently for the Egyptians and Israelites.

_____

_____

_____

_____

Using "God's Presence in the Trial" as a guide, compare the *angel of God* and Jesus Christ?

_____

_____

_____

_____

Based on what you've learned about the *angel of God* and *pillar of cloud*, why do you think Rob calls Rule #7 *Envision God's enveloping presence?*

_____

_____

_____

PREPARE FOR THE JOURNEY

According to these verses from the Psalms, what does God do for His people?

5:12: _____

_____

32:7: _____

_____

32:10: _____

_____

33:22: _____

_____

125:2: _____

_____

139:5: _____

Throughout the ages, where has God manifested His presence?

Exodus 40:34–35: _____

_____

1 Kings 8:10–11: _____

_____

John 1:14: _____

_____

Ephesians 2:19: _____

_____

What do these verses teach about the presence of God in your life?

Matthew 28:20: _____

_____

John 14:18–21: _____

_____

1 Corinthians 6:19: _____

_____

According to John 11:32, what impact did Mary believe Jesus' presence would have had in her family's crisis?

_____

_____

_____

_____

PROCEED ON THE JOURNEY

How would having Jesus right beside you affect your response to the challenges in your life?

_____

_____

_____

As we've seen, the Bible indeed teaches that the presence of the Lord is as near to us as our very breath. The question before us, though, is how to be aware of His presence.

Rob offers four suggestions for practicing the presence of God. Rewrite each suggestion in your own words and record one practical application of each as you face your Red Sea.

Affirm His nearness in your heart.

_____

_____

_____

Visualize God's presence in your mind.

_____

_____

_____

Access God's nearness through prayer.

_____

_____

_____

Reflect His presence in your demeanor.

_____

_____

_____

_____

PONDER THE JOURNEY

In light of Rule #7, record a journal entry that includes reactions and your intended response to what you've learned. Blank journal pages are provided for Step #7 beginning on Page 77 in the back of this study guide.

Heavenly Father,

Sometimes as I go through the tests and trials of life, I feel so alone. I now see that You are indeed near me. I can't go anywhere outside of Your presence. I am asking You to help me sense Your nearness. As long as You're near what do I have to fear?

In Jesus' name, Amen

As the mountains surround Jerusalem, so the LORD surrounds his people, from this time forth and forevermore. (NKJV)

Psalm 125:2

RULE #8

Trust God to deliver in His own unique way.

So you're in the midst of a crisis. Perhaps your initial, natural reactions were fear, panic, and an attempt to gain control or give up. Yet, you've taken a deep breath and committed to follow The Red Sea Rules to get you through:

- You realize God means for you to be where you are.

- You're more concerned for God's glory than your relief.

- You're acknowledging your enemy, but keeping your eyes on the Lord.

- You're praying.

- You're staying calm and confident and giving God time to work.

- You're taking the next logical step by faith.

- You're envisioning God's enveloping presence.

You're taking one step at a time as you journey through your Red Sea. Of course, whether verbally or mentally, you must be asking, *Is God going to do anything here?*

Rob, who bases his answer on Scripture, emphatically replies, *Yes!* So he encourages us to take the next step, which is Rule #8:

Trust God to deliver in His own unique way.

On a scale of 1 to 10 with 1 being *no faith* and 10 being *great faith*, how confident are you God is going to act in the midst of your Red Sea? Explain your answer.

_____

_____

_____

_____

PREVIEW THE JOURNEY

Read Rule #8 in *The Red Sea Rules*.

Read Exodus 14:21–29.

Imagine you're an eyewitness to the parting of the Red Sea. Tell your story to the reporter.

_____

_____

_____

What were the Israelites thinking and feeling before their rescue?

_____

_____

_____

Let's assume after Moses calmed them down, the Israelites believed God would deliver them. Do you think they imagined the "parting of the sea method of deliverance"? Why or why not?

_____

_____

_____

What did the Israelites have to "do" to "get God" to divide the waters on their behalf? Explain your answer.

_____

_____

_____

Rewrite Rule #8 in your own words.

_____

_____

_____

_____

PREPARE FOR THE JOURNEY

Summarize what these verses teach about God's deliverance: Deuteronomy 23:14; Psalm 34:19; Psalm 50:15; 2 Timothy 4:18.

_____

_____

_____

_____

Are the promises regarding deliverance just for people in the Bible or do they apply today? Explain your answer.

_____

_____

_____

_____

Define the three ways Rob suggests that God delivers His people:

Miraculous Ways: _____

_____

Providential Ways: _____

_____

Mysterious Ways: _____

_____

If you personally know of a miraculous way God has used to deliver you or an acquaintance, please describe it.

_____

_____

_____

_____

Do you agree or disagree with Rob's statement:

> *Though miracles still occur, God uses them sparingly. Even in Scripture, miracles were not God's standard operating procedure.*

_____

_____

_____

Do you see providential ways of deliverance in Philippians 1:12–18? Why or why not?

_____

_____

_____

Were John the Baptist (Matthew 14:1–12) and Stephen (Acts 7:54–60) delivered? Why or why not?

_____

_____

_____

How do you reconcile Psalm 34:19 and Hebrews 11:35–40?

_____

_____

_____

_____

Are mysterious ways of deliverance actually deliverance? Why or why not?

_____

_____

_____

_____

Rewrite Isaiah 55:8 in your own words.

_____

_____

_____

PROCEED ON THE JOURNEY

In your current Red Sea have you witnessed any miraculous, providential, and / or mysterious ways of deliverance? Explain.

_____

_____

_____

_____

How can you recognize or prepare yourself for the unique way God chooses to deliver you?

_____

_____

_____

_____

Draft a note to God regarding your expectations for deliverance. Please read Job 1:20–22 and Daniel 3:16–17 before you write it.

_____

_____

_____

_____

PONDER THE JOURNEY

In light of Rule #8, record a journal entry that includes reactions and your intended response to what you've learned. Blank journal pages are provided for Step #8 beginning on Page 79 in the back of this study guide.

Heavenly Father,

I confess that I want relief. I want the problem fixed according to my limited vision. But I'm learning Your ways are not my ways. Grant me wisdom to see my Red Sea and Your method of deliverance from Your viewpoint. Give me ears to hear, eyes to see, and a heart to trust what You are doing in my life.

In Jesus' name, Amen.

"For My thoughts are not your thoughts, Nor are your ways My ways," says the LORD. (NKJV)

Isaiah 55:8

RULE #9

View your current crisis as a faith builder for the future.

As a young Christian, when problems pounded me, I dragged myself to my pastor and mentor looking for help. After hearing the same sad stories several times, Rob counseled me:

> *I don't know if this is going to encourage or discourage you, but get used to problems. They're not going away. Everything you face now is preparing you for something else in the future. God is trying to develop faith in you. If you don't learn it now you'll face the same test over and over again until you do.*

It has been over 30 years, but I have never forgotten that lesson, which is actually Rule #9, the next step on our journey:

View your current crisis as a faith builder for the future.

As you contemplate your journey through The Red Sea thus far, has your faith in God increased, decreased, or stayed the same? Explain.

_____

_____

_____

PREVIEW THE JOURNEY

Read pages Rule #9 in *The Red Sea Rules*.

Read Exodus 14:30–31 several times.

What did God's people learn about Him after crossing the Red Sea?

_____

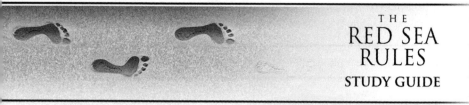

After crossing through the Red Sea on dry land, the Israelites *feared the Lord* and *believed in the Lord*.

What does it mean to *fear the Lord*?

_____

_____

_____

List some synonyms for *believe*.

_____

_____

_____

What does it mean to *believe in the Lord*?

_____

_____

_____

Is there a relationship between *fear* and *faith*? Is it important that *fear* precedes *faith*?

_____

_____

_____

_____

Relate the following statements to the *fear* and *faith* of the Israelites:

> *Faith is only as valuable as the object in which it's placed. Walking with great faith on thin ice leaves you cold and wet. Walking with weak faith on thick ice leaves you safe and dry.*

_____

_____

_____

_____

Ideally the Red Sea episode should have been a faith-building experience for the Israelites. Surely they would trust God with great faith when they faced another trial in life.

According to Exodus 15:22–24, did God's people exercise great faith during their next test? Why do you think they didn't?

_____

_____

_____

Does this continuous building of faith in the Israelites encourage or discourage you? Why?

_____

_____

_____

Rewrite Rule #9 in your own words.

_____

_____

_____

PREPARE FOR THE JOURNEY

Based on 2 Corinthians 1:8–9, what's one of the reasons God allows trials into our lives?

_____

_____

_____

Reread "Treadmills for the Soul", then write a definition of faith in your own words.

_____

_____

_____

Read the account of Jesus calming the storm in Matthew 8:23–27. What was the disciples' reaction when they saw the storm?

_____

_____

In Matthew 8:3, 13, 16, what had the disciples witnessed Jesus do prior to getting in the boat?

_____

_____

_____

How do you reconcile what they previously witnessed with their lack of faith?

_____

_____

_____

According to James 1:2–4 do you believe faith-building through problems is a process or a one-time act? Explain.

_____

_____

_____

_____

PROCEED ON THE JOURNEY

What are you learning about God, the object of your faith, as you walk through your Red Sea?

_____

_____

_____

How is your increased knowledge of *who God is* and *what God does* affecting your faith?

_____

_____

_____

_____

As you face your current faith-building Red Sea, what might God be preparing you for?

_____

_____

_____

_____

Is there anything you may need to relearn in your next Red Sea? Explain.

_____

_____

_____

_____

PONDER THE JOURNEY

In light of Rule #9, record a journal entry that includes reactions and your intended response to what you've learned. Blank journal pages are provided for Step #9 beginning on Page 81 in the back of this study guide.

Heavenly Father,

I don't know all of the reasons I'm facing my current crisis, but I do know this: You want to reveal Yourself to me in a deeper and clearer way in the midst of it. I pray because of this trial, I will know You better than I did before I experienced it. I believe Father. Help my unbelief. Increase my faith in You.

In Jesus' name, Amen.

Yes, we had the sentence of death in ourselves, that we should not trust in ourselves but in God who raises the dead. (NKJV)

2 Corinthians 1:9

RULE #10

Don't forget to praise Him.

Several weeks ago, on a rain-slicked road, a driver lost control of his vehicle, veered into my son's lane, and totaled both cars. The next day my uninjured, yet dejected son, lamented, *Dad what am I going to do? I know my car is old, but it's dependable. I can't afford a new one and the insurance company will never give me enough money to get another car like that.* Well, my son just called informing me the insurance company offered him twice what he thought he would get for his "used" vehicle. He was ecstatic! He excitedly summarized the entire episode, *Dad, my bad day has turned into a great day. Thank God!*

Unbeknownst to him, he just took a step through the Red Sea by implementing Rule #10:

Don't forget to praise Him.

It has been a long, perhaps painful and tearful journey through our Red Sea. We started off honestly identifying our current crisis and reaction to it. Panic, fear, and a desire to control the situation were the norm. We've learned to recognize the sovereignty and providence of God through it all. We're now calming down, resting in His presence, faithfully praying, and taking action steps only as He directs. We know regardless of God's specific methods of deliverance, He's building our faith for His grand purpose.

It's now time to stop. Reflect on God's character. And respond to Him in praise, worship, and adoration!

Thus far in the journey have you been praising God? If so, for what?

_____

_____

_____

_____

PREVIEW THE JOURNEY

Read Rule #10 in *The Red Sea Rules*.

Read Exodus 15:1–21.

After safely crossing the Red Sea, the Israelites stopped to praise God. Define the verbs used in Exodus 15:1–2 (NKJV) to describe their actions of worship:

Sing:_____

_____

Praise:_____

_____

Exalt: _____

_____

As you read carefully you'll discover they praised God both for *who He is* and *what He did*. From the following Exodus 15 verses, record why the Israelites praised God. Circle the ones referring to *who God is* and double underline the ones referring to *what God did*:

1._____

_____

2._____

_____

3._____

_____

4–5. _____

_____

6. _____

_____

7. _____

_____

11. _____

_____

13. _____

_____

16. _____

_____

18. _____

_____

21. _____

_____

Summarize what you learned about God from their praise.

_____

_____

_____

Summarize what you learned about praising God from their praise.

_____

_____

_____

All throughout Scripture we find both exhortations to praise God and examples of praising God. Slowly read through Psalms 100 and 150 and then record your impressions about praise.

_____

_____

_____

_____

God is deserving of praise at all times, but in our journey we're specifically focusing on praise during times of testing. Such praise should occur before the deliverance, during the crisis, and after the crisis. Read the following passages and indicate when the praise occurred (before, during, or after) as well as other insights about praise you glean:

Acts 16:25–32: _____

_____

Job 1:21–22: _____

_____

Luke 17:11–19: _____

_____

In the Luke 17:11–19 passage 10 lepers were healed, but only one praised and thanked God. Why do think there's a tendency to neglect praise and thanksgiving?

_____

_____

_____

Rob expressed disappointment for the occasional lack of praise even in his own church. He then commented, *Maybe we need a crisis.* What does he mean?

_____

_____

_____

_____

What do you learn about the relationship between praise and problems from Jonah 2:7?

_____

_____

_____

_____

PROCEED ON THE JOURNEY

Right now, pause and record why you should be praising God in the midst of your journey through your Red Sea.

_____

_____

_____

_____

Rob offers several suggestions for developing a habit of praise. Record an action step you can take to implement each suggestion:

Begin the day with praise: _____

_____

Use your car-time for praise: _____

_____

Incorporate praise into the daily quiet-time: _____

_____

Praise God in the assembly of a church: _____

Develop a perspective of praise: _____

_____

_____

_____

PONDER THE JOURNEY

In light of Rule #10, record a journal entry that includes reactions and your intended response to what you've learned. Blank journal pages are provided for Step #10 beginning on Page 83 in the back of this study guide.

Heavenly Father,

I want to be like the one healed leper who praised You and not like the nine who didn't. You are worthy of praise for who You are and what You do. Great are you Lord and worthy of praise. Right now Lord I praise You for how You're showing Yourself faithful in the midst of my Red Sea. Thank You for what You are doing in me through this crisis.

In Jesus name, Amen.

Enter into His gates with thanksgiving, And into His courts with praise. Be thankful to Him, and bless His name. (NKJV)

Psalm 100:4

RULE #1

_____

_____

_____

_____

_____

_____

_____

_____

_____

_____

_____

_____

_____

_____

_____

_____

_____

_____

_____

_____

_____

_____

_____

_____

_____

_____

_____

RULE #2

_____

_____

_____

_____

_____

_____

_____

_____

_____

_____

_____

_____

_____

_____

_____

_____

_____

_____

_____

_____

_____

_____

_____

_____

_____

_____

_____

_____

_____

_____

_____

_____

_____

_____

_____

_____

_____

_____

_____

_____

_____

_____

_____

_____

_____

_____

_____

_____

_____

_____

_____

_____

_____

_____

_____

_____

RULE #3

_____

_____

_____

_____

_____

_____

_____

_____

_____

_____

_____

_____

_____

_____

_____

_____

_____

_____

_____

_____

_____

_____

_____

_____

_____

_____

_____

_____

_____

_____

RULE #4

RULE #5

RULE #6

RULE #7

_____

_____

_____

_____

_____

_____

_____

_____

_____

_____

_____

_____

_____

_____

_____

_____

_____

_____

_____

_____

_____

_____

_____

_____

_____

_____

_____

_____

_____

_____

RULE #8

_____

_____

_____

_____

_____

_____

_____

_____

_____

_____

_____

_____

_____

_____

_____

_____

_____

_____

_____

_____

_____

_____

_____

_____

_____

_____

_____

_____

_____

_____

_____

RULE #9

_____

_____

_____

_____

_____

_____

_____

_____

_____

_____

_____

_____

_____

_____

_____

_____

_____

_____

_____

_____

_____

_____

_____

_____

_____

_____

_____

RULE #10